Blind Insights
into the
Writing Process

Richard Krause

Fomite
Burlington, VT

Copyright © 2022 Richard Krause
Cover Art: Dan Stone
Author Photo: Atsuko Sakai

All rights reserved. No part of this book may be reproduced in any form or by any means without the prior written consent of the publisher, except in the case of brief quotations used in reviews and certain other noncommercial uses permitted by copyright law.

ISBN-13: 978-1-953236-64-7
Library of Congress Control Number: requested
Fomite
58 Peru Street
Burlington, VT 05401
www.fomitepress.com

02/24/2022

Also by Richard Krause

Studies in Insignificance
Optical Biases
Eye Exams
The Horror of the Ordinary
Crawl Space & Other Stories of Limited Maneuverability

Acknowledgements

Some of these epigrams and prose poems have appeared in the *Wisconsin Review, California Quarterly, Portland Review, The Prose Poem, Asylum Annual,* and *FragLit*.

I am grateful to Marc Estrin for his editing, for the original idea for this collection, and for taking a chance on my work.

Contents

Preface	1
Because I Write Blind	3
Writing Is Wanting to Take People in Hand	3
I Can Never Write What I Want	4
Throw Insight to the Winds	4
I Stop Writing Rather Than Be Interrupted	5
Forced to Accept Yourself	5
Your Writing's Too Tame	6
Writing Means Going Down Swinging	6
He Gets Up at Five Every Morning to Write	7
EPIGRAMS I	9
If I Could Write What I Want, It'd Be a Howl	35
We Write Books Because We Are Crippled	35
Writing to Gain Fame	36
When the Work Doesn't Come, I Bully It	36
My Writing Is Designed to Humiliate Me	37
Imagining a Crucifixion Writing	37
Intentionally Writing What Is Abstruse	38
I Don't Believe in Writing, Only in Rushes of Thought	38
Hearing the Same Story about Charley	39

EPIGRAMS II	41
Poetry Requires Patience	76
Imagine Pottery in Poetry	76
RILKE Taken off My Hands	77
Spraying the Pages of a Book	77
My Attitude toward Cripples	78
His Lisp Is Why He Went to Sea	78
How the Ego Works	79
Letter Writing	80
My Nightmare	81
The Little Indian Girl Plays Cards	81
You Thought That Illegitimacy Has a Chance	82
Being Rewarded for a Lifetime of Work	82
About the Author	85

Preface

That this book was even contemplated suggests there are few texts answering what the writing process is beyond those addressing customary tips and techniques. Marc Estrin had the idea that writing groups and classes that "want some insight into the brain-itineraries they are courting" might benefit from such a book. This work is not intentionally prescriptive, but hints at insights into the throes of writing. There is no map for insight, least of all sight that by its nature covers everything and nothing. Insight is something privileged. I don't claim it, yet it is part of my work that comes because I am there and looking. I don't know how, hence the groping each morning with the attendant reach, that is blind. The claims I make are not visible entrances, but involve what is so beyond me that it is humbling, almost degrading for my having such limited control. Oedipus's vision starts blind. A book suggesting anything else is imposed, a handbook of techniques that leads the way not by demonstrated findings that I imagine these unintended epigrams and paragraphs are. They occurred to me putting in the effort and time. They are essentially beyond me, just as the creative process is, if they are honest, beyond anyone. You reach it blindly, unexpectedly with enough doubt, will, pertinacity, and confidence. If you don't recognize the extra sight, you'll not get there. This is a book of such sightings, beyond the terrestrial landscape of everyday vision that as rich as it is often gets in the way of true access. These insights came about without conscious calculation, almost beyond effort; they are the result of blind, unashamed reaching.

Because I Write Blind

Because I write blind, with the fury and outrage of not seeing what I am doing, of not having eyes to tell me the way, I dash and spill ink blindly, knock things over, sentence patterns, rigidity; it is a huge cyclopean anger, a one mental eye that knows the epic is there, something Homeric inside, and its outrage is that it must travel blind to it as the poet, the bungling giant he knows he might become, escapes from himself by something nobler, by better instincts through the ignominy of putting its own eye out with an implement as hot as the imagination. Again and again the poet blinds himself, for every act of writing is over the outrage of not seeing.

Writing Is Wanting to Take People in Hand

Writing is no more than wanting to take people in hand. The only excuse for being occupied with writing is that we don't know how to grab people in any other way. Instead of holding them we take the pen and place it gently on the paper adding softest stroke after stroke, caressing and working towards our deepest meaning, then finally being carried away with passion as the strokes lengthen almost to illegibility. We've consummated our efforts, but still the people are unheld, even if all the strokes are made.

I Can Never Write What I Want

What dismays me is that I can never write what I want, something intentional. Everything is happenstance, has more control of me than I do of it. I am at its mercy, its beck and call, a bellhop listening for the softest tinkling from within my inner ear to respond with the most deferential phrases that say just what I want to hear, placating and smooth. Or rude at times to put the ghost of the guest in myself in its place. But always, each morning, after a good night's sleep, it is a new challenge. I never know who is going to wake up in the hotel of myself. What new personalities have checked in overnight, and who is going to depart that day. And being only a bellhop, I only have limited access to the register, and though I live alone, I never quite know who is staying with me.

Throw Insight to the Winds

Insight, what is there blind, groping in us that needs it? What larva squirming, uncomfortable without eyes that each time mistakes insight for real sight, for the indispensable elements of seeing, for the vision it pretends it is a substitute for. Rather throw insight to the winds for one day of real looking.

I Stop Writing Rather Than Be Interrupted

I stop writing early rather than be interrupted by the person I'm expecting. For every idea I write has the stamp of if not haste then of the imminence of interruption. Perhaps sentences bear the weakness of nobody ever coming, and are too lazy in expressing themselves. As much a fault as being too hurried. What is the proper pace for writing? And how much does it depend on who comes, or who stays away?

Forced to Accept Yourself

You have almost to be forced to accept yourself. Put your back to the wall. Hands up. That kind of surrender to be busily employed writing. None of this moleish earnestness, this getting down to work crouched, imagining a victory in intimidation. No, it has to be an open capitulation, you have to enlist yourself, assent to the physical despair of first throwing your arms up in the air. You have to strike through the eyes. What you write has to be all ice picks, but its glittery approach, its pinpoint accuracy, has to give the impression that something else is happening, something less dangerous that will not leave the reader temporarily blind to your efforts the way good writing always does.

Your Writing's Too Tame

Your writing's too tame, he told me. You have to make it feral, give it teeth, claws. Make is snarl. "But how?" By pretending it is not writing at all. Pretend there is something caged inside you that must have its freedom. But the thickest, strongest bars won't allow it. Pretend that a stick is being poked in your ribs from outside the cage. "Come on, you. Don't be so tame." Get angry. Pretend there is someone on the other side who is doing everything possible to rouse you, get your goat. What you do is get his, pounce on him, sink your teeth into his neck, let jets of blood spurt high in the air and at the very places your claws hold him. "What about the bars?" The bars! That's the point, you've forgotten them. Left them behind for just as much of your strength as you were unable to pry them apart with.

Writing Means Going Down Swinging

What writing means is going down swinging. It is pugilistic, snub-nosed; it is what in the brain comes from the wrong side of the tracks (some poverty in yourself). What writing is in the last resort is deprived. It is the desire for acquisition, gain, recognition. It is the shunned, avoided like the plague; it is what flees the body by building it up. It is workouts and sweatshops; it is the twisting out of the last drops of inspiration. It is the exhaustion of winning, the punchiness finally of not being able to read what you've written as yours, of not being able to identify your achievements. It is finally the brain damage that maunders in astonishment over having been something it is not.

He Gets Up at Five Every Morning to Write

He gets up at five every morning, he says. To write, and because his Japanese wife is asleep. And because too he's a believer in the past, he lays offerings at their house shrine and sees in the gray Tokyo mist the shrouds of spirits that he hopes to capture in his poetry. I tell him unabashedly that I make it out of bed by noon and get down to work after a big breakfast of French toast, eggs, sausage, oatmeal, and coffee, lots of it. And a piece of fruit as a concession to not having a shrine. Then a few puffs on a cigarette to create the early morning mist. Then I sit down to work after catching the news and doing the dishes. "I always sit down on an empty stomach. My mind has to be clear," he says. "That's your trouble," I say. "I glut myself so I can then clear my mind. It's like cleaning house, aided of course by my digestion, while the wife I don't have is not in bed, so I can easily make metaphors to place her there."

EPIGRAMS I

Arranging large numbers of epigrams, you want to insert some that are not so successful or epigrammatic—to leave breathing holes for the reader. If he agrees too often with you, he will begin to resent you. You must show him also your deficiencies. People never like to see only your strengths because that never allows them to employ their own.

*

The imprecision of some writers is perfectly suited to the equally imprecise minds of readers not wanting to be bound by any fixed impression of what they read.

*

Some of us write because of the absence of anyone to talk to, others as a cure for a kind of garrulousness.

*

My idea was always not to have to write anymore, to at some point have done enough. I didn't know the enforced gluttony of having to continue, the vomit couch of a life's work.

*

Some people have too much bitterness to write, others not enough.

*

My writing has become so fluid that it is almost something more than language, what I want my work to be. A freshet, a stream, finally something drenching like a cataract. But that doesn't so much drench the body as make the vision turbid. Makes for introspection to the extent that the eyesight fails reading me.

*

Whenever I do something good, I can't for a moment imagine in myself the ability, the energy, to do anything again. There is something paralyzing about work done. It is like a basilisk stare. Its very look on the page immobilizes.

*

Your metaphor gets too clever and ceases to function as any transportation of meaning, a conveyance. Instead it becomes self-sufficient, breaks off, takes you nowhere, only up and down its combustible and swaying wooden grillwork that after enough trips leaves you a little sick to your stomach, dizzy, and ready for the real ride home.

*

Sometimes it doesn't work getting it out of yourself by writing, for it then attacks you from the outside.

*

You eventually write what is on your mind, no matter how much you are misled by what you read.

*

Regarding epigrams: People want the commitment, the open failure of a poem.

*

A thought to be an epigram has to reproduce incestuously, but not give any impression of offspring.

*

A good epigram is designed to discourage further thought. It is meant not to let you think.

*

How important we consider it to have the first say, to make the initial identification; the greed over this moment is what is called originality.

*

If you accumulate enough insights, will that not in time constitute a way of looking, an optical bias that other people will think they need glasses for?

*

A criticism of my writing: the greenhouse effect of it. The airlessness. How everything is controlled. The temperature, the amount of light, the moisture to grow just what I want. But grown from life or experience, but so carefully monitored to give the impression of something other than that, something unusual and out of the ordinary, but with all the ingredients—like the square watermelon Japanese farmers grow. All the seeds are there but the perception is different.

*

Almost every writer is superstitious (you can't help it if you rely on something as tenuous as the imagination), and comes to the conclusion that people are bad luck.

*

That most of us can't write our way out of a paper bag always insults the trees they were made from, but contributes to the legends of people being trapped inside.

*

Dedication is when—like an animal caught in the trap of other people's admiration—you are willing to gnaw your leg off, willing to sacrifice one paw to defend your freedom. It is no more than a dedication to cunning. Or maybe it is the craft that you put in your work that you can then lean on like a cane that has functions more varied than the one leg.

*

Forcing people to read my work or listen to me read is like pulling teeth. But I play the dentist just to leave them toothless, gumming what I have to say.

*

The need to write something you are proud of abases.

*

People are always looking for antecedents to what you do because they don't trust originality enough to even participate in its expression by reading you.

*

People will nit-pick your work, and that's OK if they are trying to improve some dropped stitch, if there is an error in design or craftsmanship. But not if they are trying to delouse it, that you won't stand for. That kind of lice discomfort in your writing is what gives it value, what makes people—even though they'd never admit it—itch for more.

*

I rely on what I have written like a bed of feathers; what I haven't written, however, torments me like dead geese I myself will have to pluck if I want a continued sense of comfort.

*

People build a mastaba about themselves, then cry writer's block.

*

Every triumph demonstrates a loss of intelligence that accumulates like mad when even moderate failure occurs.

*

There is a vigilant kind of intelligence that always stands guard over misinformation, and as a result doesn't allow even one original idea to pass.

*

The deficiency I most quickly see in artists is not a lack of talent so much as the absence of the kind of intelligence that would make the talent almost unnecessary.

*

Genius is little more than finding your way out of the maze of intelligence, little more than a rat's work.

*

In the absence of a love life, one feels almost compelled to exaggerate the relationships between words.

*

The advantage of being a thinker and not a poet is that you can better pretend to ignore inspiration. A thinker mistakenly imagines he can think anything he wants—it is this mistake that he almost unfailingly turns to advantage, to thought.

*

The idea will always quietly free itself from someone who lingers over the right word.

*

It is curious how our thoughts seem to come out of the emptiness they are trying to fill.

*

There is a gap between thoughts that makes the teeth visible.

*

Nothing can deplete thought so much as too much correctness of language.

*

We will punctuate a thought with a physical sensation when we aren't able to complete it.

*

Most people's thoughts, just like their sentences, are overpunctuated.

*

Our mental life has a contemporaneity that our physical life tries to chronicle. Maybe we live or die according to the thoughts we have, and it is only these that the body participates in when it thinks it is living.

*

I remember he asked me if I didn't like people, unaware as he was that he was witnessing the birth of an intellectual life—which always begins with the refusal of people (they are replaced by ideas)— gradually, however, hands reach out through the ideas, then arms and legs, then a head or two, and soon whole people appear again.

*

You imagine you'd meet the intellectual equivalent of the beauty you're seeking, but then realize that'd be impossible. That the intellect, especially on the same body, would in a moment be at the jugular vein of that beauty. The intellect would of course make all the customary excuses—that it was only trying to heighten the beauty even more, till its paleness from loss of blood became a shadow of its former self; in short, acquired all the perfection of a thought.

*

For some people thinking is winking, no more than connivance.

*

Sometimes the fine points of your thinking are apt by people's disregard of them to get broken off and become jagged, catching their attention that way.

*

There is a concentration that needs diluting to think.

*

Pedagogically, we claim to want to get people to think, when what we really want is for them to think about us.

*

Cleverness is rarely party to the large swindles that pass for wisdom.

*

The held-in-reserve quality about brilliance is its intermittence. Steady, unabated brilliance is no more than glare.

*

Nothing blows brilliance to the wind like caution.

*

I want to be less of a psychologist than one who is able to trick people, and more of a psychologist than one who is tricked by them.

*

There is something necessarily blinding about insight, and a peculiar clarity of vision to oversight.

*

To make light of insight goes a long way towards establishing the illuminating atmosphere necessary for it.

*

Most people's attention span involves little more than a salute.

*

People who don't have the antennas to understand make up for it with mandibles that devour nonstop.

*

What's in the back of our mind frequently has a broken vertebra, and can't move.

*

Lately contraries, contradictions, leap too eagerly into my mind. They don't develop, they are there already, or a trick of language drawing from the negative places them there too easily for them to be beyond suspicion of not having truth value.

*

The rapidity with which the mind works is destined to slow the gait down, even to the point of inventing more of a club foot than anybody needs for reflection.

*

Most people never realize that the benefit of being on intimate terms with their mind is the unfaithfulness that allows.

*

The best minds know just what tasks to apply their imaginations to, while inferior minds are imaginative about everything.

*

Sometimes my mind becomes clearer when I am tied or otherwise awkwardly bound because it is free of the coordination of my body.

*

Feeling doesn't require talent, but can make the greatest talent blush for lack of it.

*

As long as you think what is precious is precise, your feelings will always be cameo.

*

In her speech, she said the boy she tutored pinched her. Even though they couldn't feel the pinches themselves, her mentioning them riveted the judges' attention to her white arms where they gave her high marks for the bruises they hadn't been able to make.

*

All schools of art should be little more than one room, and have a potbellied stove as their instructor.

*

Sustaining a work of art is like sustaining an erection, only the wooden gods can do it indefinitely.

*

Artists that at some point don't cut off their nose to spite their face probably aren't worth identifying.

*

Some people are artists out of a poverty of emotion. They draw the very nudes they can't embrace.

*

There is a difference between art as catharsis, and trying to wash your dirty laundry in it. The latter is possible, but only by those whose motives are spotless.

*

A lame emotion often gets rehabilitated in poetry, for all art is a kind of prosthesis.

*

I walk behind very fat people in imitation of their waddling, and gather in their wake the stares on the street. Pretty soon it is only I who am watched, the person having disappeared into my own antics. There is something in this of the artist who imitates, copies nature. The artist in the spotlight, left alone on stage, the anomaly having disappeared, with only its imitation—himself—to be looked at.

*

We are given all the ingredients to turn on ourselves, all the ophidian suppleness to devour what there is about us that we can't swallow. There is a supersense in art that absorbs what life would otherwise plague us with, predatory instincts that are clearing the road of those dead portions of ourselves that if left lying would add up to a corpse of living, instead of a body of art.

*

Talent is the great manipulator. It is the ultimate persuasion, the five-finger discount; it makes the rest of us all seem to be wearing mittens.

*

Anything followed to its logical absurdity will produce more talent than the average person possesses.

*

Often talent is no more than growing free of the netting only we perceive. It is due to a special facility for imagining ourselves trapped.

*

People want their own talents codified, passed into law, so that everyone will be compelled to follow what they are gifted at.

*

Nothing paralyzes like being well thought of, or gives you quite the freedom of a bad reputation.

*

One day you will get your deserts and will be cloyed, and will quickly realize how much better it is to devour yourself in the main and most inspirational meal of unappreciation.

*

What you have to do is balance yourself on the humpback of someone's disregard of you. Make of its deformity a dromedary, something graceful spanning deserts.

*

Despising people is a reaction to their not giving us our due. It is one way we ourselves can reward merit.

*

The passion some people have for accumulating and cataloguing their own failures leads you to suspect that privately they also consider them a kind of success.

*

We overwhelm people and then are left more bereft. Better the quiet respect they associate with unostentatious failure.

*

Half your energy is taken up with the idea that you are not properly appreciated, the other half with how to divert attention from the appreciation of others.

*

There are times when I succumb and want to sell myself, attract people. But there are other times when I want no buyers, when I want to make the merchandise of myself so thoroughly my own that it is unpurchasable, even defective.

*

He pretends not to be able to read his own handwriting so as to give people the opportunity to include him in the efforts they have not made.

*

"Success sucks," he said. And you knew exactly what he meant. Words you wouldn't have used, but to which you could attach that deep drawing meaning to something that takes more life than it gives.

*

"Connections, connections," the cynic says convincing you that you'd rather endure the pain of a dangling nerve than this society of false synapses.

*

The so-called successful are not necessarily the more talented, but those who have better endured their "untalent." That's what's difficult for a person with any sensitivity. Talent is common, universal. Having the rough edges, the insensitivity to overcome the talent you don't have is rare and what makes for success. Though of course not the success that overcomes the talent you do have.

*

We want so much to differentiate ourselves from others, but without losing the advantage of a favorable comparison.

*

Some people never develop simply because they refuse to outgrow the appreciation of those they care about.

*

Some people want a monopoly on appreciation, believing that alone will keep it from accumulating elsewhere.

*

What if the limelight that you thought illumination was, was only a lemon—the bright color it gave off? Would you turn sour over that, or would you bask in that false light like it was part of some stage, and the applause wasn't the silent explosions of acid out of each of its pores—but hands clapping, or an unpuckered sucking of the lips over your performance?

*

I can't believe after a frenzied outburst of applause that the audience doesn't as much want to hear itself.

*

Talent has to surpass ambition, ambition talent. Both have to be left by the wayside like the snake grown enamored of its tail in its own mouth. Only then can genius go striding off free and easy with the monkey on its back behaving like the master.

*

The easiest way to bury your talent is to condemn society for not providing mine shafts, cranes, bores, drills, except at a price you can't afford. Most writers don't accept their poverty and build from there. Instead they would rather dream about contractors cheating them.

*

The first step towards someone being what they truly are is a reluctance toward it. They need something to get in the way, something to surpass. Perhaps the less talented are only those who find fewer obstacles in themselves, i.e., have less to overcome. Those who to all appearances have the grace and ease to do anything they want. The very qualities that belie saltatory, springing capacities that would elevate them out of mere gracefulness.

*

The sense of failure learns not even to pass water when it is not convenient for others. Success, on the other hand, is always incontinent.

*

Why do we not resent some people's talent, while the mere suggestion of it in others has us running for cover?

*

If you truly think you have something to say, invariably it is to render other people silent.

*

Some people are so naturally what you try to be that your twenty studied steps only equal their one stride, or the careless placement of their foot.

*

There is a name for everything. What there seems to be no name for is only changing or between names.

*

To be always questioning the meaning of what you write deprives it of the significance of not being followed.

*

His speech is so soft that you want to shake him to somehow give bite to what he says. Get him to openly masticate the language, dribble, drool down the sides of his mouth, spit out the words, hiss his meaning, something that would bring out the snake in him, and the mongoose in you.

*

Small talk forces us from the great conversations with ourselves.

*

Beware of the mumbler who just because of indistinct speech says what everybody wants to hear.

*

When we interpret people as making silent judgments on us, frequently it is only our own unvoiced estimates of ourselves.

*

Speaking out of the side of your mouth is the opposite of looking out of the corner of your eye. In the one you are trying to deceive, in the other not be deceived.

*

What is said cannot convince some people unless it was first heard at a whisper.

*

That silence that discourages being broken up into conversation is often pieced together by it.

*

Often we will invent arguments or prolong differences of opinion just for companionship.

*

The care people take in being correct is never mistaken for imagination.

*

We have no one word to describe the opposite of a thief. That's because the opposite is not eluding us, or on the run.

*

"I keep my word," he says. "That's your problem," I say. "Your vocabulary is too limited."

*

There is a word play that shows the absence of deeper amusement.

*

We mistrust people who misuse words, just as we do those who use them too well.

*

Without platitudes we'd have to mouth original speech that would eventually make us unintelligible to one another.

*

The pretense of meaning is half the signification.

*

There has been something systematic about what I don't know being gradually uncovered, that doesn't even notice what I do know being concealed again.

*

The comments of the government reach all the way inside us with the long arm of artificial insemination that pretends to be the real bull.

*

Originality is coming back from the ashes again and again. It is not meant to be a charcoal crow, a decoy duck. It is what starts the longest flight only when the most feathers are plucked. Originality is what exposes.

*

If I Could Write What I Want, It'd Be a Howl

If I could ever write what I want it would be a howl, a cry, a shriek. What I do write is muffled, a concession to not truly letting loose. Art is such a false, devious way of expressing ourselves. It is such a meekness, that you can't help despising the first person that thought of it. The duplicator. Who hadn't the courage that first time to express himself. Instead, he settled for art, mincing his way to the truth. It is a bad habit not to submit to the more human alternative to be loved outright for what we are. What a circuitous, mechanical route art is. Who takes it? Who would in fact choose to duplicate feelings if he had the courage to express real ones? Who but the weak, the fainthearted.

We Write Books Because We Are Crippled

The proof that we are crippled is that we write books. The lame hand on the pen. What shaking must have preceded the first shape. What twisting of the body, what disfiguring. Who in good health could have wanted to make an a? What freedom of body movement must have been given up. What patience and ill-health, what lack of vitality it must have required. Where must the desire for running, for motion have gone that caused the first man to write, and what malice, what jaundiced notions must have danced round his head? What secret pleasure he must have taken! How much hatred of his fellow man must have prompted him to give healthy arms and legs the braces, the twistings of language.

Writing to Gain Fame

To gain fame, success, I used to think was the goal of writing. But only in my most superficial moments when talking to someone who doesn't understand me at all. In fact, I enjoy doing the work more than anything, get the reason for my existence from it. It gives stability, structure to who I am. Otherwise every day, every year that I am older, collapses without meaning. My effort to write gives weight to the collapse.

When the Work Doesn't Come, I Bully It

There is a stubborn pertinacity when the work doesn't come. I bully it, gore it, bloody myself tripping over my own cape. I create in fact the stands of applause, all the boos against myself. I am what clamors for my undoing at the same time I am readying the sharpest horn, the roundest, most distended belly that it will pierce, and the matchstick legs that the most muscular bullneck will lift with hardly an effort for all the crowd to see. Then the four hooves of feet of myself will trample what I have not done for all to observe. That will be my triumph, as well as my defeat.

My Writing Is Designed to Humiliate Me

I never do things I am proud of. Almost always they are ignoble. It is as if my writing is designed to humiliate me, bring me to my knees. Could that be ultimately its secret intention, and nothing I really have to say? And when it does seem high-minded, noble, is that not because I'm only unwittingly setting myself up for a revelation that is not base enough by itself, but needs something ostensibly higher to come toppling down on it?

Imagining a Crucifixion Writing

We create because there is something in ourselves we want to tack down. Something drifting like smoke that hasn't the substance to be pierced. But we imagine a crucifixion nonetheless. Imagine hands and feet, and that we can spear through the side of what we want to say. And finally, crown it with thorns that will make the blood run in the reader, who out of sympathy will be compelled to identification. So heated will our reader become that he'll cry for water. Instead we'll give him gall.

Intentionally Writing What Is Abstruse

A writer intentionally writing what is abstruse. "This will get them!" he says, as he buries his meaning even further—It even sounds good to me, he reflects—and doesn't take the trouble to explicate it. "So much the better," he says. "It will give me depth! Let them excavate. Here, I'll put this sentence in as a pick. Give them that much shining clarity, tantalize them about the rest. Or this sentence, I'll make the wooden handle, and over here a little solid ground. For after all the mundane must have somewhere to stand!"

I Don't Believe in Writing, Only in Rushes of Thought

Finally, I don't believe in writing, but only in rushes of thought, images, clusters of associations waiting to be picked, that dry in an acceleration of time the moment we aren't ready for them. Writing? Only scribblers do that, Egyptians whose grand legends of the hereafter bespoke of infertility. What they had scribes for (and scarabs and cats). To take down everything that couldn't be written. That they couldn't create without a fiction! We capture nothing writing. Almost always it hunts us.

Hearing the Same Story about Charley

She didn't want to hear the same story about Charley, she said. So before the car would arrive, she'd tell Helen to prepare what she was going to talk about. Not the same story. Helen would instead be tongue-tied, frozen speechless thinking all the more the little scrap of narrative about Charley that she could now, following the instructions of her sister, no longer tell. Eventually she became absent-minded because the one story on the tip of her tongue could not relieve itself periodically and loosen the rest of the memories that its telling would have invariably produced.

EPIGRAMS II

Few are given the satisfaction that what they write will grab people by the throat. It is tragic considering all the long necks there are in the world that never get strangled.

*

SHAKESPEARE had all the horror he needed at his fingertips so that he could dig into even an infant's skull as if its soft fontanelle was a window of opportunity.

*

What if we all are what's not even funny, and that alone is the reason for our emphasis on humor?

*

There is enough cant in what I write to slip unawares into almost any posture of sincerity.

*

You garner the attention for yourself, then what? No more pleasure lurking in the shadows calculating when your time will come. What a powerful loss is almost any recognition at all.

*

Talent sometimes ties your hands so tightly that only an escape artist could develop it.

*

All the beauty of Nature—and where was BECKETT but trapped in a stunning unappreciation of it cluttered with two or three men, and one disposable woman.

*

For true talent silence is the best applause.

*

Some people have too much intelligence to create, others not enough.

*

EMERSON, as well attuned as he was to society, was in the end out of place in his church, in his family, and even in his friendship with THOREAU; he was so thoroughly alone that he almost didn't know what to do with himself but each time write his way brilliantly out of it.

*

WHITMAN triumphed with only modest talent by being himself.

*

The smugness of someone who writes epigrams is insufferable, except when they are not very good.

*

When we were youths he'd laugh at my achieving "posthumous fame," ignoring the lifelong satisfaction of being unrecognized but knowing your value.

*

There is enough talent to distribute to others, but still the gifted hoard it.

*

DOSTOYEVSKY is the unnecessary underside of SHAKESPEARE, who didn't need any.

*

The vast gap between people, especially for NIETZSCHE, was illustrated by his imagining the sweetest grapes were picked out just for him.

*

SHAKESPEARE is not there in his creations, but we are.

*

The stunning reach of SHAKESPEARE outdistanced that of nature, even when he collaborated with it most famously in Lear.

*

The most remarkable aspect of creation is not the universe, the sheer beauty of occupied space, nor is it the animal world, or the simple existence of man, but it is, despite all his brutality, a simple act of kindness absolutely unconcerned with its own interest.

*

Is there nothing that overlooks our own interest about us?

*

Is the reason for accomplishment to make other people feel bad just underneath the good it makes you feel?

*

We all are strangers to ourselves that we think we should know.

*

To look ourselves in the face mostly requires glasses and a fake moustache.

*

He said, yes, I could one day write like HESSE, and now, fifty years later, I realize he probably answered that way because he was attracted to me. On the other hand, it kept me going a lifetime, little different than the pig bones that CHAUCER's Pardoner passed off as relics of actual saints.

*

KAFKA was never arrogant, but so sure of himself that arrogance almost looks like unnecessary timidity.

*

THOMAS MANN's home is the one BRECHT was most likely to break into.

*

Something accurate but with no tension in the twist is lost to the world that only wants observations that spring back at it.

*

What makes your jaw drop is the start of a ventriloquist's dream that you will have nothing to say for yourself.

*

There is something static about BECKETT that he takes, like no one else, full advantage of when his characters do move.

*

We want recognition. It is our protoplasmic revenge for seven pounds of being born without an ounce of input.

*

He'd rather incinerate himself than all the books in the library, he says, until I tell him we all have a least one book in us, which gives him pause.

*

ORWELL knew himself just enough to make his honesty powerful. Any more or less would have significantly weakened his rhetoric.

*

The literalist trips over his own feet, then serves them up to someone else, pickled.

*

To think God is any more than our exaggerated power of narrative is to reduce him even further to nonexistence.

*

All true poets are blind, and have to find a way to disavow their interfering vision.

*

He was always taking inventory of his talents and as a result never developed them.

*

BRECHT looks out for himself by including everyone else with such a matchless clarity of intent that, though you want to, you can't imagine he has anything up his sleeve but the public good.

*

To do work that takes people's breath away is little more than the wax museum you want to put everyone in anyway.

*

Art is clever for how successfully it can sidestep our objections to losing interest in ourselves.

*

What boredom if I have to live even one morning without ambition.

*

You stake your claim to a language that since childhood you felt wanted to burn you at it.

*

Ability is universal, but its development is idiosyncratic.

*

Artists fed by their interior life suffer more malnutrition.

*

What hides your talent best is just the ordinary world that has no need of it.

*

You get the feeling BECKETT's characters are looking out the basement on all of France as depicted by BALZAC. But, like the legless boy in GORKY's "Hobgoblins," they are never able to leave their subterranean confines with even a fraction of DOSTOYEVSKY's brilliance.

*

Of creativity we are simply weak vessels just bearing the storms above us hoping that lightning strikes. Who could possibly be proud of such powerlessness?

*

Anyone after truth will become easily diverted by a love for language. For that reason, we have to avoid the right word.

*

All the metaphors regarding the pen being mightier than the sword only indicate a lack of courage in picking up a weapon to defend ourselves with.

*

Talent allows everything else to be overlooked, though the tendency is to gaze on that everything else to avoid admitting what we weren't born with.

*

Because we don't know that what we do is good, we dream of when we were children, and being good was a substitute for it.

*

To have no agenda but the truth is to appeal to the deaf, dumb, and blind. It is a world unto itself that will be recognized only on its own terms by those least equipped to understand it.

*

There is something so freeing about futility that loosens the grip on the whip every moment is.

*

Being uncomfortable with praise is often the result of the anger behind having had to wait for it all your life.

*

Jealousy is the key to all interaction and pulls us down without our even knowing it, like a tiger an antelope no one notices missing from the herd.

*

The best response to people overlooking value is to simply overlook them by creating more of it.

*

What if, when you get inside all truths, you find that nothing is original that doesn't pertain to you?

*

You can almost see the feeling in the very eye of the rhino with the enormous head and giant horn. Its look conveys the question of how they got there and is answered only by the thickest neck that says it doesn't matter now that I have to carry them.

*

What does anything mean but what we are, and the infinite variations on that.

*

Mathematicians' days are numbered only when they have no access to metaphor.

*

Is it any coincidence that my fountain pens are made in Germany, Italy, and Japan?

*

We say "my intelligence" when it is almost the least proprietary thing about us.

*

POE didn't need to love people because he was so lodged in their alimentary canal by way of the most developed brain, that in the end he couldn't even digest himself.

*

Is there any worse abandonment but to be left behind by what you do?

*

The art of placing yourself last is lost because everyone wants to win, and no one realizes the strategic advantage of having someone ahead of them.

*

While some people are victims of their own talent, others are almost triumphant in not having any.

*

A tortoise so well defines itself that we have to bring in the hare as its opposite, and even foolishly instigate a race that ends counterintuitively, to show how reliably unreliable language is with the slow outdistancing the fast.

*

SHAKESPEARE is so expert at insults and put downs that his verbal bullying seems almost comic, but at the same time the essence and purpose of language.

*

The trick is not to give away what you don't know. Epigrams do that by the sheer monopoly they endeavor to secure over what you do know.

*

You know when people have been diminished by your talent, but don't quite know when that talent diminishes you.

*

The disarming honesty of just being yourself is at the same time boring. In fact, we almost expect ourselves to dissemble to keep our own interest.

*

He cultivates with what some call near brilliance his talent for not having any.

*

The claim that the French made POE better must massage some deep ache in them that POE's long transatlantic fingers could not reach.

*

Communication teachers imagine sincerity is not disarming only because it can't be taught.

*

Just looking at a porcupine, you know it is a failure of flight, not to mention the compromised writing capacity of the quills still on its body.

*

There is a compensatory squinting when people open up to you.

*

People who don't read do read the world around them, which is a decent substitute, while people who do read are often blind to their surroundings.

*

Word play deprives most people of physical activity so should never be encouraged in children.

*

Lucidity is deadly and blinds us with too much clarity so that we are vulnerable from all sides at once.

*

The black and white anomaly of the orca makes you desperate in your own life to categorize the two colors into equal right and wrong. The orcas are a confusion until they kill another handler. Only then can you take sides against their being held in captivity.

*

What you know about holds you in a captivity ignorance never does.

*

Rocket science will always be in its infancy compared to human emotions.

*

Few are so in love with themselves that they get carried away over the threshold and can double as both bride and groom.

*

What occurs to you sometimes falls from a sky not there, but from an overhead of our own making whose absence of stars doesn't even bother us.

*

Our love of books sometimes ends in one being thrown at us.

*

I wisely avoided taking the apartment by the ocean, fearing that the sounds of the waves would interrupt my thinking now that I got what I wanted.

*

To always know what people are thinking constantly interferes with your own originality.

*

We don't deserve POE, and I suspect that the sheer difficulty of his private life demonstrated that he didn't deserve himself either.

*

When things fall into place you don't know where to put yourself. Yet you are there handling yourself like a sausage that would make anyone gag.

*

All the power of literature is the human race caparisoned like a beautiful horse no one can ride.

*

Most intelligence is shared vision that can't accept the momentary blindness of going its own way.

*

CONRAD is a wonderful target for knowing so much about so little of himself.

*

You are someone who doesn't need disguises, but involuntarily thinks about them to get away with the perfect crime you don't even know you have a desire to commit.

*

Any action is always partially an act. There is no pure behavior when the mind is involved.

*

He felt so much a doormat to his own intellect that even his thoughts could wipe their feet on him before they went anywhere.

*

The infinite compassion of DICKENS made some of his characters a transparent evil through which he could still see himself.

*

We couldn't live without euphemisms. Calling a spade a spade would dig right into our chests and enlist the use of someone's foot pushing that tool deeper into us.

*

If silence could speak, it would say no more than we do.

*

Art is what silences the crowd, the rabble, from otherwise breaking up the furniture. It keeps us from destroying wherever we are at.

*

In the end, antlers rule.

*

Oh, for someone, anyone to talk to that appreciates your work, but then you realize you just have to do more of it so that it carries on a dialogue with itself.

*

All the power we get not caring about people makes us equal to nature and every one of its laws governing us.

*

We all have voice boxes we will be placed inside of by anyone who listens to us speaking where they imagine the sweeter sound is our banging to get out.

*

The best thoughts are not thought out but, like Johnny-on-the-spot, are unintended collaborations of name and place.

*

THOMAS MANN was impacted, but irrigated too by all those canals he found in Venice.

*

We can only imagine what people say behind our backs, but everything is behind our back if we are going anywhere.

*

No matter the development of the mind, the world will always be there as if its very existence has its own ideas.

*

It is not easy to intend to write an insight. It is so out of your hands that it might as well be in anyone else's.

*

We are so helpless starting out, and can end up absolutely ruthless. Who could connect the two but by poisonous fangs hidden somewhere in those snakes we don't quite take ourselves to be.

*

Get to know yourself and that is your death knell. All you can do is approach it like the ringing of bells in a distant monastery and know that you don't want to identify who the inevitable monk with strong hands is.

*

Defeating others is so superficial that deep thinkers often become tacticians at losing.

*

The pickpocket is selective about what he steals. He is the artist most of us are not, who take throughout our lives whatever we can, rarely having the decency to keep it hidden.

*

Not to be diminished by someone else's talent is a good sign that yours will develop.

*

Writing is the best excuse not to submit to the so-called perverse desire to actually expose ourselves in public.

*

The lamb following Mary to school is immune to being eaten, but is still food for thought.

*

The pleasure of hindering people comes from not admitting the obstacles we are to ourselves.

*

We don't have enough respect for people, but if we did we'd never create anything.

*

For FLANNERY O'CONNOR, peacocks must have put human beings in perspective, so she viewed them without the worshipful eye she saved for her birds.

*

You don't know the value of what you do beyond your own excitement. In the end, value is really determined by the impression you make on yourself.

*

The certainty of the hawk just sitting on the fence impresses me. Had I half its confidence the problem of this mouse-ridden world would be solved.

*

I reread my work before someone else I know reads it, trying to determine its worth for them through me.

*

Your thought has to be convoluted enough to establish itself as yours, but at the same time have clarity and punch so that someone might be hit hard enough to actually fall through the ropes and clean out of any imaginary ring.

*

Our thoughts almost always move us out of the driver's seat. The best ones involve a loss of control that is regained only at the very last moment.

*

What doesn't follow often follows us to make sense of it. Everything involves such parades from one incoherence to another.

*

DICKINSON never became the butterfly she imagined, but was the pupa many times over with her distinctive examination of every aspect of our unborn existence and its ultimate focus on death.

*

Good writing is little more than not asphyxiating yourself by airing too many grievances.

*

One of the characteristics of man's intelligence is to find analogies, for he is much too alone without them.

*

To account for the still swarming insects after the treatment, the almost illiterate exterminator tells beautiful stories about the colony being overfull and the queen kicking out the excessive termites who even grow wings for that purpose.

*

BUBER enshrined the Other—what a trick to avoid the all-too-powerful self.

*

What if our powers of observation bore back into us so that we were more easily looked through for observing others?

*

Do we live in a world of our own making? Not as long as we have a mind that is not.

*

What is thinking but what we are spoon-fed, for there is something infantile and dependent about how we receive ideas.

*

Hiding in any talent is always the requisite violence to use it at the expense of others.

*

Corniness doesn't, but should envision fields of grain it can hide in.

*

To define a man as a thinker is such a dwarfed perspective, that he's left in the end as a marble statue few can relate to.

*

WILDE believed in nothing beyond the irony of the moment, and, yes, perhaps that is everything.

*

Some people draw from themselves pictures complete, even without those pencils they are free to stab others with.

*

Making your mark mostly ends up black and blue on someone else.

*

Who is not stunned by those without talent being envious of you?

*

The element of fraud in KAHLIL GIBRAN alone deepens his authenticity.

*

The whole sensate world doesn't hold a candle to one person's self-consciousness.

*

When nothing comes, you almost have to base your life on false arrivals.

*

Whatever you notice insures you will not be. Notice everything, and that will live your life for you.

*

To see through anything requires a respite of faulty vision.

*

When something is simple, I find myself almost guiltily estranged from it.

*

What homogenizes us is that we all think we are something different.

*

He lived his life too honestly not to feel himself a fraud.

*

Bandwagons are tolerable as long as the music is good.

*

Some people, to live with themselves, need to retreat inside another person.

*

If you are open to yourself, others will follow.

*

To paraphrase Iago, nobody is who they are. We are all, to the extent that we think of ourselves, always someone else.

*

The best minds often don't know it, and so are able to work uninhibited by the deadly idea of their own superiority.

*

People have to make sense, or nobody will be responsible for its manufacture.

*

How many times has the muse departed, leaving only her soiled garments?

*

There is the very thug in BRECHT that he has to beat down in society. In fact he took care of himself in his plays never to be identified.

*

The two trees barely grow on the sides that face each other, but flourish on their opposite side, suggesting that if we want to accomplish anything we have to turn our backs on those close to us.

*

Depth isn't the bottom, but the interpenetrated surface that always fools people with its reflections.

*

In cartoons, people are constantly getting hit, suggesting there is something cathartic about expressing what is not so readily permitted in real life.

*

Inside anyone someone else can be shut up. We are all the source of each other's confinement.

*

KAFKA's approach to everything was its inaccessibility. More than anything, what he couldn't reach comprised his genius.

*

If you twist yourself enough to find the truth, someone will come along and use you as a corkscrew to open the nearest bottle of wine with.

*

TWAIN probably knew he was a fraud in later life, dressed up in suits you couldn't get him into as a child.

*

The literal cleans house of the figurative. But sometimes when it gets freezing cold, there does remain one skater on the small pond left after the pipes burst.

*

Sometimes nothing tells the truth so well as a tortured syntax.

*

Some people we don't want to meet, but we do want them to hear of our successes, imagining that too will keep them at a distance.

*

Kindness bullies everyone into even unwanted resemblances of behavior.

*

"Get over yourself," someone says when there is something of you that is insurmountable in them.

*

We are left more alone by our ambitions than we realize. They stand before us like the full headdress of an American Indian whose large colored feathers come from birds we can't even begin to identify, any more than we can identify all that we haven't accomplished.

*

The lie doesn't matter so much as who is telling it. That always determines the degree of falsehood.

*

Truthtellers live with liars as if their compatibility is part of one and the same story.

*

The truth is a stiff wooden soldier, the lie like a Pinocchio that has been brought back to life.

*

So much to read, so little time, that you can't help attacking people to make the most of this desperately unbridgeable gap.

*

Most can't hold a candle to the accomplishments of others, but we can in secret burn their houses down.

*

Being honest is little more than admitting that whatever you say is always about you.

*

When people are too reasonable, the imagination is permanently on hold.

*

The problem with talent developing is that it will eventually, the more you master it, replace you.

*

How can we knowingly write a non-truth? By it not entirely being that. Nothing in fact can be anything unadded to by something else.

*

I read snatches of CHAMFORT in the Philippines between flies biting my legs. I bloody my copy of him, blackening whole letters in the effort to stop the loss of blood. But again and again I turn back to CHAMFORT, almost as often as the flies return to me.

*

What motivated VERMEER to such an absence of productivity? Just the opposite of the creation of the world, but what could that be? To freeze it in a limited number of still lifes?

*

Paradox may not win the day, but it will set people free.

*

Poetry Requires Patience

Poetry requires the patience not to pursue your meaning. Letting it float free. Letting words buoy you while you fish for rhyme, the tug and pull at your lines. But most poets, though anglers, stop with the catch. They never show the internal angling. The operculum torn free, the bleeding at the mouth, the evisceration from a line having been swallowed. They never show you the guts of the poem. What readers today never angle for.

Imagine Pottery in Poetry

Imagine if there were only pottery in poetry. At best something ceramic, glazed, if a foot of verse was only a vessel's base, something to stand on. Or if you could drop rhyme, content, meaning itself like a large vase, or pot. If that amounted to the poetry of your efforts, and nothing fired, polished, glazed. If all your efforts to kiln lines, oven metaphors, if the control of the heat of inspiration, of your working the drafts yourself and the twelve hours it took to bring out the minerals, could be nullified, scrapped, thrown on the potter's heap at the least imperfection—the poetry of that would make shards of the rhymester, or even the person looking for deeper meaning than the lines even under the heat of inspiration could ever give.

RILKE Taken off My Hands

I read *Duino Elegies* a few feet from the ocean. The print is stiff, erect, immobile in my hand, yet permeated by the salt and smell of the shore that mixes with the poetry. At each wave I imagine the ocean reaching up just after it crests and is about to curl grabbing the book from my hand, drawing it back into itself. Around and around the pages would turn. The ocean twisting and spinning what it can't make out. The book is already swimming in my brain, but the print soon gives away the meaninglessness of the ocean. The ocean, for all that the pages suggest, remains dumb, brutish, thundering, with no meaning but itself. Finally, unable to digest the book, it will toss it back on shore, or into claws that will make short work of RILKE's most spiritual lines, what took a hiatus of ten years to complete. Pages that will exercise the crop of some crab. The ocean will now have taken RILKE off my hands.

Spraying the Pages of a Book

He sits spraying the pages of the book, his mouth half filled with food, coughing as he reads. Some of the dried eel he's been eating lands on the pages and leaves spots of oil that enlarge the more he doesn't notice them. Still he reads merrily chewing, digesting the print along with the eel and an occasional swallow of coffee. It is as if turning the pages is part of his eating process and his coughing on the pages an added place the food can go to show that he doesn't have to swallow all he reads either.

My Attitude toward Cripples

I have a curious attitude toward cripples, or dwarfs, something that on first encounter appears taunting. But it is that I want to exaggerate the shortness, the limp, as if the insignificance, the imbalance will take on a weight and size that it would never have neglected and untaunted. Or perhaps, too, it is something dwarfed and disproportionate in me that I am trying to rectify by attaching myself continually to them by way of ridicule, not having access to them on an equal footing.

His Lisp Is Why He Went to Sea

His lisp is why he went to sea. Why in the wind and breezes he felt the company, the compatibility that he never found among his straight-talking species. The soughing of the sails, the flapping, the screeching of the birds that followed the ship, the fish harpooned even bore an auditory resemblance he felt to his own inability to enunciate anything but the pain of his inadequacy, his being caught, his hunger following, his own lack of destination that tacked this way and that, that veered and plummeted, that finally could tongue no more intelligibility than the wind in the very cloth that provided the impetus through life, that gave voice to an inability to be any more eloquent about his lisp and life than by giving his dysfunction the working, visible definition of being out to sea.

How the Ego Works

She talked rings around me in Japanese. I fumbled at what she tried to teach me, reached, groped for the word, like the first snowflakes that didn't stick, but melted as fast as she pronounced them. The word for "chin" and "knee" canceled themselves out in their similarity. But still she buffeted me and blew swirls of sentences around my head, little pyramids of words for "white," "lamb," accumulated. I weakened, grew tired, she waxed stronger, fell on me like a heavy blanket that I acceded to out of a vague desire for some linguistic warmth. Finally, weather-beaten, though the evening was still young, she could see that I could absorb no more sentences, that my mind was freezing, so she stopped content, my ego shivering enough, and though calm in her own mind, she heard chattering; the cold that she hid so well in our using English all the time. It was my turn, though I didn't realize it, how the ego works unconsciously combating the drift that would bury it; it was my turn, taken half unaware, in the midst of stories that she only half understood, the blitzkrieg, the avalanche of work I got out, read, now descended on her like the last steeples of a village that was fast disappearing, erasing completely the flurry of Japanese that I had been submitted to.

Letter Writing

Every time he received a letter, he wanted to answer it as soon as possible to rid himself of the answer turning itself over and over in his mind, modifying itself each time, draining his energy of thoughts that might be better applied elsewhere to some fresh insight. So quickly would he begin to answer letters that he even misread whole passages in the haste to reply. He would construct the most careful, well-turned sentences even before the letters arrived. Finally, so overcome by the need to answer he would actually sit down and write answers to letters he never received; so great was his need to get caught up, that when the letter did come it would almost be unanswerable, for in some cases having already been answered not once but twice in real letters. Soon, however, his anxiety about being the least bit behind in his correspondence was conveyed to others as they started to receive his letters before they could answer. He had written enough letters to insure no response. Letters to his friends piled up so that they—the sheer length of them alone which would have discouraged a response—didn't know where to begin. The burden had shifted to them. Now *they* were the ones behind, and it was *he* who finally found peace of mind.

My Nightmare

My nightmare: that I'd be living with my wife in our trailer. That I'd fail the doctorate exam. We'd both have a good cry over it. Then she'd lead me into our bedroom. We'd make love. It'd all come out, the disappointment, the frustration, the humiliation. And just when I'd think it'd be all right it'd occur to her to ask, "But what'll I tell my friends?" This nightmare recurs, even though I have no wife and there are no exams to pass.

The Little Indian Girl Plays Cards

It strikes me the way the little Indian girl plays cards with her brother on the train. The way she hugs so delicately a whole handful to herself gives away how closely and similarly to her breast she'll hold the infidelities of her lover or husband, that she'll be too gentle to stop having received practice playing cards as a child with her brother who I can tell she is more fond of than to stop his cheating.

You Thought That Illegitimacy Has a Chance

You thought that illegitimacy has a chance, but it's passed around. At first very carefully, swaddled, the same as any other child. No one knows the disease is spreading. The baby looks like any other. It's not. People start to avoid it as something contagious. First the father, or mother, soon both. First one family takes it. Relations visit. After all, there is some acknowledgement. It's not legal, but there is blood. But blood thins and soon the child is left with family after family. Bi was so attractive, what happened, why didn't BRECHT stay with her, only fathered her illegitimate child and fled. He kept coming back, but, no, finally they both left him. At sixteen to the German Army. Eight years later he was dead on the Russian front. Legitimately dead.

Being Rewarded for a Lifetime of Work

The trick is getting over the expectation that you should be rewarded for a lifetime of work. A comment of admiration, a few newspaper articles, a few roomfuls of people gathered expressly to honor that work. How much of your efforts does that add up to? Nothing to speak of or mention. Rather you should get past that. What you want is nothing people can plan for. No articles, no acceptance, no gatherings—you have stopped bringing your writing to poetry readings. What you want is so much of yourself gathering unnoticed that when it does strike out of the blue it is like lightning, that it carries

About the Author

Richard Krause has had three collections of fiction published titled *Studies in Insignificance* (Livingston Press, 2003), *The Horror of the Ordinary* (Unsolicited Press, 2019), and *Crawl Space & Other Stories of Limited Maneuverability* (Unsolicited Press, 2021). He also has had two collections of epigrams published, *Optical Biases* (EyeCorner Press in Denmark, 2012) and *Eye Exams* (Propertius Press, 2019). Krause lived for nine years in Japan and drove a taxi for five years in NYC. He currently lives in Kentucky where he is retired from teaching at a community college.

More Odd Birds from Fomite (books that are hard to classify)...

Micheal Breiner — *the way none of this happened*
Roger Coleman — *The World Was Late*
Bill Davis — *Cheap Gestures*
J. C. Ellefson — *Under the Influence: Shouting Out to Walt*
Stephen J. Goldberg — *Rants Raves & Ricochets*
David Ross Gunn — *Cautionary Chronicles*
Andrei Guriuanu &Teknari — *The Darkest City*
Andrei Guriuanu &Teknari — *Portraits of Time*
Gail Holst-Warhaft — *The Fall of Athens*
Daniil Kharms — *Connections* (translator Roger Lebovitz,
　　　　artist Delia Robinson)
Roger Lebovitz — *A Guide to the Western Slopes and
　　　　the Outlying Area*
Roger Lebovitz — *Twenty-two Instructions for Near Survival*
Pippo Lionni — *Fat Facts of Life*
dug Nap— *Artsy Fartsy*
dug Nap— *Friends*
Delia Bell Robinson — *A Shirtwaist Story*
Rosen, Ken & Wilson, Richard — *Gomorrah*
Claire Russell — *Dear Mr. Thoreau*
Peter Schumann — *A Child's Deprimer*
Peter Schumann — *All*
Peter Schumann — *All, Nothing, Nothing at All*
Peter Schumann — *Bedsheet Mitigations*
Peter Schumann — *Belligerent & Not So Belligerent Slogans*
Peter Schumann — *Bread & Sentences*
Peter Schumann — *Declaration of Light*
Peter Schumann — *Diagonal Man Theory + Praxis, One and Two*
Peter Schumann — *Erbarme dich - Have Mercy*
Peter Schumann — *Es is vollbracht - Mission Accomplished*
Peter Schumann — *Faust 3*
Peter Schumann — *Handouts and Obligations*
Peter Schumann — *Life and Death of Charlotte Salomon*
Peter Schumann — *Planet Kasper, One and Two*
Peter & Elka Schumann — *She Sits, She Rides, She Flies*
Peter Schumann — *We*
Schütz, Heinrich — *Notes of Devastation*
M.D. Usher & T. Motley — *Poem A Mashup*
Writing a review on social media sites for readers will help the prog-

that much shock, jolt, that people will not have time even to appreciate it. Rather they will be floored by it. What you want is work that they don't have the time to read. But not from its being boring, or uninteresting, or their not having time, but rather because the work itself, the build-up of energy, of electricity, didn't give them time. That even though they were finally willing to pick it up, they were more quickly struck down.

ress of independent publishing. To submit a review, go to the book page on any of the sites and follow the links for reviews. Books from independent presses rely on reader-to-reader communications.

For more information or to order any of our books, visit:
http://www.fomitepress.com/our-books.html

www.ingramcontent.com/pod-product-compliance
Lightning Source LLC
Chambersburg PA
CBHW071505070526
44578CB00001B/448